YOUR KNOWLEDGE HAS VALUE

Juliana Vianna da Nobrega

Regional Integration in Europe and Latin America

A Comparison of events and theoretical approaches

GRIN Verlag

Bibliografische Information der Deutschen Nationalbibliothek:

Die Deutsche Bibliothek verzeichnet diese Publikation in der Deutschen National-
bibliografie; detaillierte bibliografische Daten sind im Internet über http://dnb.d-
nb.de/ abrufbar.

Imprint:

Copyright © 2012 GRIN Verlag GmbH
Druck und Bindung: Books on Demand GmbH, Norderstedt Germany
ISBN: 978-3-656-34153-6

This book at GRIN:

http://www.grin.com/en/e-book/206830/regional-integration-in-europe-and-latin-
america

GRIN - Your knowledge has value

Der GRIN Verlag publiziert seit 1998 wissenschaftliche Arbeiten von Studenten, Hochschullehrern und anderen Akademikern als eBook und gedrucktes Buch. Die Verlagswebsite www.grin.com ist die ideale Plattform zur Veröffentlichung von Hausarbeiten, Abschlussarbeiten, wissenschaftlichen Aufsätzen, Dissertationen und Fachbüchern.

Visit us on the internet:

http://www.grin.com/

http://www.facebook.com/grincom

http://www.twitter.com/grin_com

Regional Integration in Europe and Latin America
A Comparison of events and theoretical approaches

12th April, 2012
Otto von Guericke University Magdeburg
Peace and Conflict Studies
Debates on European Integration

Juliana Nobrega

Contents

1. Introduction.. 3

2. Basic notions and general information with respect to the topic.. 4

3. Regional integration processes in Europe and Latin America – A historical outline................ 5

4. Regional integration processes in Europe and Latin America – Strengths and weaknesses 9

5. Integration Theorists on integration in Europe and Latin America...................................... 12

6. Summary and Conclusion 17

Bibliography.. 19

1. Introduction

The European integration has been in progress since shortly after the Second World War. Already in 1946, the British Prime Minister Winston Churchill held a speech in Zurich and within this speech he expressed the idea of France and Germany as the constituting countries of a European Union. At this time, the patriotic French press was outraged about this idea. But already in 1949 the Council of Europe was founded, and only two years later in 1951 the European Community for Steel and Coal was created and became effective in 1952. In 1957, the member states of the ECSC signed the Treaty of Rome to start the European Economic Community (EEC) (Schmuck, n.a.).

The European integration has been a unique process (Rosamond, 2006, S. 450) that lead also to a separate field of studies, the European integration studies. Even though Europe is unique and the integration process that has been taken place there is unique as well, efforts to compare the process in Europe with integration processes in other regions of the world were undertaken. I will tackle the matter with this regard. This paper will be concerned with the integration process in Europe compared to integration processes in Latin America. My motivation to do this arises from the fact that I am a Brazilian student and thus have a Latin American origin and I am studying in Germany, which is in my opinion and most probably not only in my opinion the most important constituting country of the European Union. It is not only the biggest economy in Europe but it is also one of the few constituting states of the predecessor of the EU already mentioned ECSC and the EEC. A second fact, which is in my opinion intuitive, is the one what the differences of integration processes are and how those can be explained. The first world with Europe and the third world with Latin America might show different difficulties and challenges with respect to efforts on regional integration.

To restate more in detail the intention of this work: The regional integration processes in Europe and in Latin America will be compared and at the same time the theories that were created with the integration processes - trying to explain them - will be brought into context with the processes. For Europe the regional integration process or processes, if one wants to divide them into different phases, are those that led to the European Union and beyond, and for Latin America one can tag the results of the processes Mercado Común del Sur (MERCOSUR) and Central American Integration System (SICA (Sistema de la Integración Centroamericana)).

The structure of this paper will be as follows: In the first part basic notions will be explained that are deemed to be important for the further text. After this, the integration processes in Europe and in Latin America will be presented with the help of major events that are seen to be constituting events – thus events that are seen to be major steps in the development of the integration process. Following this historical outline, the processes will be compared in terms of what their strengths and weaknesses are. It should be found out why integration has been gone that far or not. This will be followed by outlining the theories that were developed to explain regional integration processes. It is the intention to find out what those theories intended or could explain especially with respect to the question whether they are and can be used in different regional contexts – theories developed for Europe applied on Latin America or vice versa.

The methodology used to work out the paper is basically literature research whereas sources from the different continents were used. Key words and fundamental information will be explained in the following chapter.

2. Basic notions and general information with respect to the topic

Regional integration. Regional integration is a term already used, but it should also be explained here to avoid misunderstandings. As will be shown, there is not a single definition but various. It is not the purpose to make a clear cut and entirely explaining definition for integration. In the context of this work the following definition is more a guideline of what is meant with integration. This guideline is sufficient for the understanding of the following. Eilstrup-Sangiovanni (2006, p. 7 f.),[1] in the book "Debates on European Integration", reviews scholars of various integration theorists and their understanding of what integration is. Ernst Haas sees integration as a "process whereby political actors in several distinct national settings are persuaded to shift their loyalties, expectations and political activities towards a new centre, whose institutions possess or demand jurisdiction over the pre-existing national states" (Eilstrup-Sangiovanni, 2006, p. 7). There is a variety of definitions also due to the variety of the matters that could be integrated or integrating. Those matters could be economic ones, whereas integration could mean economic unification, or political matters and then one would talk about political unification. The creation of political institutions at the community level or ideas and opinions are also used to create a definition of integration (Eilstrup-Sangiovanni, 2006, p. 8). In this paper, integration will also be seen as a process and not as a condition for the reason Ernst Haas mentioned: It is hardly

---

[1] For an additional categorization see (Wiener & Diez, 2003).

possible to distinguish between the situation prior to a state of integration and what happened to get into this state (Eilstrup-Sangiovanni, 2006, p. 7). Thus seeing it as a process seems to be more suitable and so it will be done in this paper. Furthermore, the definition given by Haas will be the reference for the notion integration.

Context to International Relations (IR). International relations, which is a very broad field including many sciences such as economics, psychology, sociology and more (Viotti & Kauppi, 2009, S. 2) is often referred to together with integration studies. As broad as international relations are defined or can be defined, the study of European integration can be seen as a "subfield of the study of IR" (Eilstrup-Sangiovanni, 2006, p. 12). But it has to be noted that a problem with the generalization of results from European integration studies might occur, since Europe can be seen as a unique case (Eilstrup-Sangiovanni, 2006, p. 10). This will also be discussed in the course of the paper. Even if this view, that European integration studies is a subfield of IR, is not shared, as a minimum, both fields are very close and share lots of the same theoretical background. One sentence from Eilstrup-Sangiovanni (2006, p. 33) further shows the relation of the fields of study: "At a time when the discipline of IR seemed fixed on the notion that conflict was the beginning and the end of the subject matter IR, integration theorists drew attention to collaboration for welfare ends as an important aspect of contemporary interstate organization". Thus, if European integration studies is not seen as a subfield of IR, it lent its ideas to IR, and with that, both kinds of studies strongly overlap. This can be seen just through observing the theoretical approaches that are applied. Those are the same in both cases[2].

The next chapter is dedicated to presenting the integration processes in Europe resulting in the European Union and in Latin America resulting in MERCOSUR and SICA.

3. Regional integration processes in Europe and Latin America – A historical outline

The regional integration processes will be summarized shortly in the following. The resulting organizations here are the European Union (EU) for Europe, which arose from the European Economic Community, and for Central America we have the SICA and Central American Common Market (CACM), which is one of several subsystems - the economic subsystem - of SICA. For South America MERCOSUR is

---

[2] Compare for example (Viotti & Kauppi, 2009) International Relations Theory, where constructivism, institutionalism and functionalism are explained. The same theoretical approaches can be found in (Eilstrup-Sangiovanni, 2006) Debates on European Integration.

the name of the economic integrational body, which arose from the Latin American Trade Association (LAFTA) and its successor the Latin American Integration Association (ALADI), which will be shown in the following. The European Union has currently 27[3] member states whereas Germany, France, Italy, Belgium, Luxembourg and the Netherlands were the constituting countries of the predecessor organization of 1952 (European Union). SICA has seven member states with five states constituting the predecessor organization in 1951, Costa Rica, El Salvador, Guatemala, Honduras and Nicaragua, and two additional states with Belize and Panama (SICA Central American Integration System). MERCOSUR has four full members with Argentina, Brazil, Paraguay and Uruguay, whereas Venezuela has a pending full membership and Bolivia, Chile, Colombia, Ecuador and Peru are associate members (BBC News).

a) The 1940s until the 1950s

Europe. As initially mentioned, the European Union has its origins in the time short after the Second World War. The British Prime Minister Winston Churchill held a speech in Zurich in 1946. He stated his idea of a European Union with France and Germany as the constituting countries, which was not taken very seriously by the press. Shortly afterwards in 1949, the Council of Europe was founded, and only two years later in 1951 the European Community for Steel and Coal was created and became effective in 1952. The United States were a major influencing factor that brought the integration process forward. It can be assumed with a high probability that without the U.S. the integration would most have taken much longer and would not be as it is today regarding to its size and contents that form part of the union. This support was intended to strengthen the counter weight against the Soviet Union. In 1957, the member states of the ECSC signed the Treaty of Rome to start the European Economic Community (EEC) (Schmuck, n.a.). Together with the EURATOM, the European Atomic Energy Community, the three communities were called the European Communities. The articles one to three of the treaty lay down what this community intended to reach: a common market with all its aspects such as the abolishment of import and export restrictions and tariffs among members and a common policy regarding these issues towards third countries.

Latin America. In Latin America there were some attempts for political integration already in the 19th century. Simón Bolívar, the Venezuelan Liberator, expressed his idea of a unified Hispanoamerica

---

3 The member states of the EU with the year of entry are Austria (1995), Belgium (1952), Bulgaria (2007), Cyprus (2004), Czech Republic (2004), Denmark (1973), Estonia (2004), Finland (1995), France (1952), Germany (1952), Greece (1981), Hungary (2004), Ireland (1973), Italy (1952), Latvia (2004), Lithuania (2004), Luxembourg (1952), Malta (2004), Netherlands (1952), Poland (2004), Portugal (1986), Romania (2007), Slovakia (2004), Slovenia (2004), Spain (1986), Sweden (1995) and United Kingdom (1973).

following the example of the US. But history went another way. Most former colonies could not maintain their territories except Mexico and Brazil, which mainly kept it. Only after the second world war ECLA`s proposal was fruitful with the initiation of CACM for Central America and LAFTA for South America.

The origins of the Integration System of Central America (SICA) where CACM is a part of it can be found in the Charter of San Salvador, which was initiated in 1951 by the creation of a predecessor organization - the Organization of Central American States (ODECA). The integration was furthered in the 1950s with several treaties and the installation of its headquarters in 1956 in San Salvador. The Multilateral Agreement on Free Trade and Central American Economic Integration was signed in 1958 to establish a free trade area within ten years (SICE - Foreign Trade Information System).

b) 1960s until the 1980s

Europe. In the 1960s further steps with regard to integration were undertaken in Europe. A common agricultural policy was established and later in 1960s all tariffs were completely abolished. In 1967 the three European communities were laid together and then had common executive organs. In 1972 a currency mechanism was introduced to allow for stable exchange rates in the EEC. Two years later, a fund to support less prosperous regions was created. In the 1980s Greece, Portugal and Spain – all of them former dictatorships - joined the European Community. In 1986, the rights of the European Parliament were extent and a plan to harmonize the legislation of European Community states with respect to trade laws was set up. At the end of the 1980s, the community of the Warsaw Pact states started to crumble (Das Gesicht Europas wandelt sich – Fall der Berliner Mauer, n.a.).

Latin America. In 1960, El Salvador, Guatemala, Honduras, and Nicaragua signed the General Treaty on Central American Integration which initiated the Central American Common Market (CAMC) (SICE - Foreign Trade Information System). Within five years a common market and a customs union should be created. Costa Rica joined in 1964.

With respect to MERCOSUR, in 1960, with the Treaty of Montevideo the Latin American Free Trade Association was founded. Article 2 of the Treaty determined a 12 year period to implement the treaty. In 1980, again in Montevideo, the new treaty had the goal of economic integration and turned the Latin American Free Trade Association (LAFTA) into the Latin American Integration Association (ALADI). 11 countries formed the association: Argentina, Bolivia, Brazil, Chile, Colombia, Ecuador, Mexico, Paraguay, Peru, Uruguay and Venezuela. According to the first article of the Treaty of Montevideo the contracting

7

parties pursued a "harmonious and balanced socio-economic development of the region" and the "long-term objective of such process shall be the gradual and progressive establishment of a Latin American common market".

c) From the 1990s onwards

Europe. Finally, in 1992, with the Treaty of Maastricht, the term EEC was replaced by the term European Community (EC). So the EEC existed further named EC. Additionally the European Union was created whereas the EC was one of the three columns of the EU[4]. The new community exceeded that of a pure economically interested community. For example article B of the Treaty of Maastricht (Treaty on the European Union) says that a common foreign and security policy will be implemented. In the 1990s, more big steps were made within the EU: the Treaty of Amsterdam with the European citizenship, the expansion towards Eastern Europe and the introduction of the European currency. Treaty establishing a Constitution for Europe (TCE) was drafted in 2004. But it remained ungratified because of several rejections and replaced in 2007 by the Treaty of Lisbon, which included changes compared to the constitutional treaty.

Latin America. SICA was established in 1991 with the Protocol of Tegucigalpa. It contains several subsystems with special focuses on political, economic, social, cultural, and environmental issues, whereas the CACM remains to be the economic system.

MERCOSUR was constituted in 1991 with the Treaty of Asunción. It built in the treaty of Montevideo were the Latin American Free Trade Area (LAFTA) was turned into the Association for Latin American Integration (ALADI). The founding countries were Brazil, Paraguay, Uruguay and Argentina and the treaty should become effective in 1994 (compare Tratado para la Constitución den Mercado Común entre la Republica Argentina, la Republica Federativa del Brasil, la Republica del Paraguay y la Republica oriental del Paraguay). The constituting treaty is dedicated to free economic interchange, with the harmonization of national laws towards this goal until 1994 and the foundation of decision making bodies for the member states. Those were the Consejo del Mercado Común (Council), the highest decision making body (Article 10) and the Grupo Mercado Común, which is made up of ministers of the exterior and of the economy (Article 11). They are to come together when there is a need and at least once a year the presidents of the member states have to be there as well. The presidency of the council is determined on a rotational basis and for six months each turn. The Grupo Mercado Común is the

---

[4] The EC was the economic column of the EU. The other two were the common foreign and security policy and cooperation in police work and justice (Aufteilung der Zuständigkeiten innerhalb der Europäischen Union, n.a.).

working level, which can be further subdivided according to the tasks that have to be fulfilled. In the treaty itself, there are 10 subgroups listed that are only concerned with economic matters. Further protocols were signed in the following years: in 1994 the Protocolo de Ouro Preto (administrative structure) [5], in 1998 the Protocolo de Ushuaia (assures that all member states are democraties). In 2005 the Protocolo Constitutivo del Parlamento del MERCOSUR was an important step leading to the creation of a parliament.

Up to this point one can see that Europe and Latin America have been undergoing regional integration processes that started after the Second World War and aimed as a minimum at economic integration with a free trade zone and the abolishment of tariffs. Europe has been going further than the Latin American integration efforts with respect to economic integration (for example the currency union) and several organizations that go beyond a purely economic union. Furthermore, it exceeds the other organizations in size with 27 countries and complexity. The Central American integration process SICA also goes beyond a purely economic union, which is represented by the CACM. But it does not have the level of integration as the EU. Finally MERCOSUR is almost purely an economic union although other aspects have been emphasized in the recent past and a parliament is created.

The next chapter should clarify what the achievements of the integration processes have been and where they have stayed beyond expectations or beyond the achievements of comparable processes. With this respect the EU seems to be a good benchmark as an upper level of integration.

4. Regional integration processes in Europe and Latin America – Strengths and weaknesses

The history of the major integration processes on Europe and in Latin America was already presented. Now it is of interest to which extent the integration took place. Many treaties were made and organs were created on the continents, and all of the objectives sound rather similar. The questions are whether Latin America has reached a comparable level of integration compared to the European Union, how successful the integration was (if success can be measured) and what the major issues are.

Rueda-Junquera (2006, p. 14 f.) notes that the European experience showed that there are costs and benefits of the integration process but with overall net benefits. But it is also admitted that there are

---

[5] Article 1 of the Protocolo Adicional al Tratado de Asunción sobre la Estructura del Mercosur – Protocolo de Ouro Preto – shows all of the main organs of MERCOSUR.

winners and losers of the process. Since industries in some areas can suffer through abandoning trade barriers the EU established funds to transfer money to unfavored regions. Such solidarity cannot be found in the CACM.

In the EU a very developed intraregional trade takes place meaning imports and exports within the EU and among EU countries. In turn, in the CACM those relations are weak. In the EU 60% of total trade went over intra EU borders whereas in the CACM showed only 26.7% exports and 13.5% of imports on average during 2000 and 2004. For Central American countries cross-border trade with countries out of the integrated area is more important (Rueda-Junquera, 2006, S. 15). For example the US are the principal trading partners with 40% of the imports to the CACM in 2005 (Rueda-Junquera, 2006, S. 16).

Rueda-Junquera (2006, p. 12 f.) found that Central America has been lacking the political commitment towards its regional integration process, whereas in Europe this commitment was there. In cases of perceived or actual conflicts between national and regional objectives Central American governments prioritized their own objectives. For these states it has been impossible to sufficiently share sovereignty, costs and measures of integration. The legal framework of the CACM (basically the Protocol of Tegucigalpa from 1991) presents five limitations compared with the legal frameworks that constitute the EU:

1. The CACM framework is in a significant legal disorder without homogeneous and compulsory deadlines for national implementation of what was agreed upon. That led to delays and partial adoption of the framework. For example, Costa Rica has not yet agreed upon the Constitutive Treaty of the Central American Parliament of 1986 and Costa Rica, Guatemala and Panama have not agreed upon the Statute of the Central American Court of Justice of 1992.

2. The highest decision maker is the Summit of Central American Presidents. With this entity the decision making process strongly depends on the political situation of each country and that in turn is likely to slow down the integration process. A supranational body would be a better means to rapidly remove trade barriers and harmonize integration.

3. A clear leadership of one or a group of countries in Central America cannot be identified. This could have led to a faster integration process with orientation for the remaining countries to follow those guiding group of states.

10

4. The governments' credibility must be doubted about mutually since compliance with agreed upon points of the Presidential Summits was hardly there. This in turn reflects on the mutual commitment and the seriousness with which the process is regarded.

5. Unrealistic objectives and an overly complexity and high number of institutions have been hindering the integration process in Central America.

If one takes intraregional trade as a measure of the success of the CACM one can observe that until the early 1980 trade rose within the area. But political problems, civil war and several shocks in the 1980s led to a re-imposition of trade restrictions and to a strong contraction of trade among the countries. Only in the 1990s with the reconsideration of the CACM and the reinitiation with the Summit of Antigua average tariffs in the region could be lowered markedly (from 45% in 1985 to 6% in 2002) and trade among the countries rebounded (SICE - Foreign Trade Information System). CACM has been successful in promoting trade and the reduction of tariffs. Nevertheless, there were several hindering circumstances up to withdrawals from the treaty because of war such as Honduras did because of the war with El Salvador, and Costa Rica, that was expelled in 1972 because of a dispute (Chapman, 1994).

MERCOSUR was also driven by many issues among the member countries. For example Brazil and Argentina had a quarrel because the Brazilian car industry became more and more competitive supported by the devaluation of the Brazilian currency. The issue between Brazil and Argentina "led many to predict the MERCOSUR's demise would shortly follow" (Gómez-Mera, 2005, S. 110). (Gómez-Mera (2005, p. 138) therefore concludes that MERCOSUR only survived because of power considerations – to strengthen the position of the constituting member especially Argentina and Brazil on the international stage. The smaller member Paraguay and Uruguay complain about restricted access to markets in Argentina and Brazil, and Venezuela has a long outstanding ratification of its membership because Paraguay has doubts about the democratic intentions of the Venezuelan President Hugo Chavez.

Both Latin American organizations have a problematic relation in appearing as one partner in negotiations with other countries or organizations. Paraguay and Uruguay were looking for bilateral trade deals outside MERCOSUR. The SICA and CACM-country Costa Rica has negotiated with Mexico, Canada and CARICOM and there are further examples for bilateral negotiations (SICE - Foreign Trade Information System), which are not allotted by the CACM.

The EU is not without disputes as well, but there were no wars such as in Central America. The current issues are according to the news the debt crisis of various member states and the discussion how far solidarity should go. Furthermore some of the stability criteria such as the limitation of government indebtness were disregarded – one of the causes of the debt crisis in the EU. Even in Europe there is a large discrepancy between the performances of different countries. The Wirtschaftswoche summarizes all these issues on its homepage (Wirtschaftswoche). Anyway, from my point of view, the integration in the EU is much more advanced. To put it more objectively, the EU has - at least for the major part – introduced a single currency, EU-law that is taken more seriously than laws in Latin America and the integration in Europe exceeds that of a purely economic objectives following organization. Examples for that are that Europe appears with a common security and defense policy. The European Forces in Bosnia are an example for that (EUFOR). Finally, the European Citizenship is another big step in the regional integration process.

SICA also goes beyond purely economic integration in emphasizing social objectives besides economic ones. But it cannot be compared with the achievements of the EU. MERCOSUR in turn is an organization that aims almost only on economic matters (Malamud, 2010, p. 643).

Until now, one can see that the EU is much more developed in terms of size measured in number member states, intraregional trade and the objectives it follows. Furthermore the complexity of the EU and its administration goes beyond that of the two Latin American organizations (different languages, many different bodies which are not only related to the economy).

5. Integration Theorists on integration in Europe and Latin America

How the regional integration has been developing on the different continents has already been shown. Scientists took up the matter to ask and try to answer different questions about the integration processes and outcomes. Those theories that were applied on Europe and finally also taken for the analysis of Latin American integration processes will be presented. Furthermore, examples of different results of their analysis will be provided.

Development of regional integration theories. An overview about regional integration theories is provided by Eilstrupp-Sangiovanni, whereas several phases with different approaches towards regional integration are delivered (Eilstrup-Sangiovanni, 2006, p. 4 f.). It is not intended and would exceed to purpose of this paper to explain all those theories. They will be summarized briefly in the following. The

12

point is that their application in Europe but especially in Latin American regional integration should be examined.

The theories of the first phase from the 1920s to the 1960s are called normative pre-integration theories. Three approaches are classified in this phase: federalism, functionalism and transactionalism. The theories focused on the question about the motivation of integration and the design and promotion of it. The matter of integration for federalism is described as intergovernmental constitutional bargaining, whereas functionalism is about the creation of international organizations, which assume important functions of nations. David Mitrany, for example, was a representative of the theory of functionalism, and his perhaps intuitive proposition was that not politicians but experts should solve the various non-political problems that occur on the national and international level (Viotti & Kauppi, 2009, p. 126). Transactionalism is described in short as learning and socializing through communication. As the name indicates transactionalism relies very much on economic principles and stresses individualism and self-interest (Encyclopedia69.com, n.a.).

The second phase, partly overlapping with the first one, started in the 1950s. It was called the phase of explanatory integration theories. Neofunctionalist and intergovernmentalist approaches were developed. They focused on solving the question on why integration takes place and how the outcome of an integration process can be explained. Neofunctionalist approaches tried to explain how economic cooperation led to a demand for political cooperation.

The third phase started in the 1980s and is named the phase of neo-institutionalist and governance approaches. Those included the new institutionalist approaches: rational, historical and sociological institutionalism. These approaches deal with institutions as intervening variables that constrain actions of self-interested actors (rational and historical institutionalism). Historical institutionalism additionally assumes that existing institutional arrangements trigger integration, so that the past constellation of institutional arrangements has a big influence on integration. The sociological institutionalism goes that far to state that institutions are fundamental for the identities and interests of actors. Comparative and governance approaches were also developed in this third phase. These approaches include informal integration apart from the easier observable formal treaties (Eilstrup-Sangiovanni, 2006, p. 3 f.).

The fourth phase started in the 1990s and is the phase of constructivist and critical perspectives. Its main focus is to answer how integration develops and how it influences the identities and interests of social actors. An important word that initially was already touched upon is the international society. In this context, socialization is deemed to take place not only with exposure to national influence but also to international ideas, norms and institutions (Eilstrup-Sangiovanni, 2006, S. 4).

Theories on Latin America and Europe. Malamud (2010, Sp. 637) states that Ernst Haas and Philippe Schmitter started in the 1960s to do research on regional integration in the CACM and the LAFTA trying to apply neofunctionalist theories there. Besides Haas Raúl Prebisch, an Argentine economist and director of the UN Economic Commission for Latin America (ECLA) in 1948, was another influential person in the field of regional integration theories for Latin America. Haas and Prebish are seen as the pioneers of integration theory in Latin America. The ECLA and neofunctionalist approaches were the first approaches to cover Latin America. They were developed in the 1950s until the 1970s. ECLA, based in Santiago de Chile, followed a historical-structuralist approach with many different topics such as structural imbalance of payments, structural inflation and regional integration. According to Haas (2006, p. 437) neofunctionalism was developed to "give the study of European integration a theoretical basis". He also stated that it was not only developed for Europe but for a general application (Haas, 2006, p. 438). Neofunctionalism assumes that states are expected to "defend their preferences and to cooperate when cooperation was deemed necessary". Domestic competition for influence trigger state preferences and those preferences are based on values. According to neofunctionalism, regional integration would occur when actors "in calculating their interests, decided to rely on the supranational institutions rather than their own governments to realize their demands" (Haas, 2006, p. 438). Furthermore, neofunctionalism assumes that regional integration is self-sustaining through the demand for additional central institutions since the existing ones were not capable of satisfying the actors' demands (Haas, 2006, p. 438). A political and functional spillover is seen to foster neofunctionalism. That means that there is an effect of economic and social integration on political integration. The first one favors the other one (Rueda-Junquera, 2006, p. 644). Haas considered the weakness of integration in Latin America caused by the inability of theorists and decision-makers to effectively communicate and the inability of theorists to persuade decision makers.

Eilstrup-Sangiovanni (2006) presents further theoretic approaches on European integration which include intergovernmentalism were Andrew Moravcsik strongly contributed to and constructivism with Jeffrey Chekel as a well known representative. Rueda-Junquera (2006, p. 647) states that the Latin American literature also turned to these approaches.

Most generally, social constructivism focuses on "the social construction of the collective rules and norms that guide political behavior" (Eilstrup-Sangiovanni, 2006, p. 393). Constructivists have the

14

objective to learn about "norms, rules and identities and how they affect the conception of ourselves and how we relate to the world" (Viotti & Kauppi, 2009, p. 277). For constructivists the world is a social structure based on many factors such as norms, rules and laws, whereas these factors can affect the identities and interests of agents. In contrast to other theories, constructivism very strongly aims at the idea of a constant change, whereas realists and even liberal and economic structuralists do not go that far. The construction and change of interests and identities is key in constructivist thinking. Furthermore, constructivist see pure objectivity as impossible, since human beings are subjective (Viotti & Kauppi, 2009, p. 277 f.). With this regard Haas "originally saw identity commonalities as irrelevant at best: 'Europe is divided by language and religion, but united by regionally similar social and economic conditions and institutions; Latin America is united merely by language and religion.'" (Rueda-Junquera, 2006, p. 648). Gómez-Mera (2005, p. 135), who took several approaches to analyze the MERCOSUR in the light of the Argentinean-Brazilian conflict in 1999, found that in MERCOSUR a common identity actually has emerged – due to a constructivist analysis. Other approaches that were included by her in the analysis led her to found that power considerations played a very strong role and that those considerations were much stronger than mutual identification of partners or friendship and other more non-material matters that constructivism promotes (Gómez-Mera, 2005, p. 138).

Also liberal intergovernmentalism found its way towards Latin American integration theories. As already stated Andrew Moravcsik has strongly contributed as a liberal intergovernmentalist for the European integration process. Sánchez Sánchez (2003) applied the intergovernmentalist approach for its analysis on the reform and limits on SICA - the Central American Integration System. He summarizes that the support of the integration by governments is triggered by their preferences which in turn follow utilitarian goals – "that is, when it reaffirms that states' national interests." Sánchez Sánchez (2003, S. 45). He states that intergovernmentalism challenges elder approaches such as realism, transactionalism and neo-functionalism, which see "regional integration as the outcome of i the hegemonic power of regional states, ii the pressure of non-state actors such as the bureaucracies of regional organizations and domestic pressure groups, iii sociological factors such as a sense of belonging and regional identity, groups' social assimilation, and iv spillover theory" (Sánchez Sánchez, 2003, p. 45). Intergovernmentalism also argues that the "regional integration process is politically dependent and that an understanding of the process requires that governments' national preferences and interests – especially those of the countries that are economically and politically strongest- be seen as independent variables" (Sánchez Sánchez, 2003, p. 46). With that he clearly cites and adopts Moravcsiks work on intergovernmentalism. Sánchez Sánchez (2003, S. 60) concludes that intergovernmentalism is an approach for analysis that is fruitful for the application on Latin America. The role of the interests of governments in the integration process are highlighted, and also asymmetrical bargaining, power and concessions shape the process. Like Moravcsik Sánchez Sánchez (2003, S. 60) concludes that "integration advances in line with the logic of the lowest common denominator. Rueda-Junquera (2006, S. 648) argues with respect to Sánchez Sánchez findings that state preferences in the EU are more liberal since they are created more through the influence of a market or civil society, whereas in Central America with the SICA and CACM and also in South America with MERCOSUR traditional power elites determine preferences.

Rueda-Junquera (2006, S. 650) concludes for the Latin American and European Integration that all approaches except constructivism lead to an equal result on how integration processes work. In Europe, he argues, transnational transactors and supranational institutions were fundamental to explain the development of European integration. In Latin America only states are of importance. He states that in Central America as well as in South America integration processes can be described as sovereignty-protective than sovereignty-sharing. That goes in line with what was stated above by Haas. Politicians are not very much influenced by theorists to support functional spillovers.

As it is obvious now, Latin America was relatively early regarded by theorists of regional integration from Latin America and from other continents for examples with Ernst Haas, who mainly worked in the field of European integration. The theories were captured by Latin American scientists and applied on Latin American integration processes. The different approaches and views through the eyes of the different theories led to valuable conclusions and pointed out the differences of the integration processes.

Rueda-Junquera (2006, S. 650 ff.) concluded that there are as a minimum five issues in which European-based theories were applied outside the EU. He as others Rosamond (2006, p. 450), points out the problem of the EU as a unique organization and that this fact hinders comparability. This is something that has been tested. Furthermore, "different dynamics of origin and operation, the impact of domestic institutions, the timing of institutionalization, and the nature of politicization" (Rueda-Junquera, 2006, p. 650) are named.

With respect to the EU as a unique organization he argues that Latin American integration efforts have been going farthest apart from the EU. This is an instance that still poses a challenge for scientists in this field. Different theories seem to be capable of explaining different phases better or worse. The application of neo-functionalism to Latin American integration revealed that functionalism is better used with explaining the processes after the union was created, while intergovernmentalism better explains the initiation of the union. Thus theories are not necessarily competing but complementary. Differences can also be found in certain persons with political power that have an impact on integration processes. In Latin America it was the ignorance against theorists which were not able to have a say in decisions and in Europe some politicians strictly followed their own line and hindered the integration process such as Charles de Gaulle and Margaret Thatcher. The foundation of institutions also influenced integration processes. An example is given with the European Court of Justice and its power to of judicial settlement compared to the court of MERCOSUR with diplomatic settlement. With regard to politicization it could be observed that in Latin America technicians had influence on integration only in the beginning (for example of LAFTA and CACM) and afterwards the processes were dominated by politicians. In the EU there is a mechanism "through which political leaders agree on general principles and leave the drafting of the detailed rules to leading national and supranational technicians" (Rueda-Junquera, 2006, p. 652 f.).

Finally, regional integration theory was applied for Europe and Latin America. To a big extent theorists used the same approaches meaning that approaches such as constructivist, neo-functionalist and intergovernmentalist approaches. It turned out that those approaches were able to identify several differences in the integration processes in Latin America and in Europe that go beyond a purely economic analysis of percentages of tariffs or interregional trade.

6. Summary and Conclusion

The intention that was initially stated was to compare the integration processes in Europe that led to the EU and those in Latin America with MERCOSUR and SICA. The comparison took place with respect to historical events that constituted the integration, an examination of the processes from a more general point of view with respect to strengths and weaknesses and an analysis of the application of integration theories on the different integration processes.

It was found that even though integration efforts started more or less at the same time short after the second world war the extent to which regional integration was achieved was very different, with the EU having the highest level of integration. That means that the EU integrated different aspects such as defense, citizenship, and a harmonization of politics not only with respect to economic objectives. But even in economic matters the EU is farthest because a common currency and a common central bank (even though not in every country) is a very big step in the direction of a common market.

Why integration was more or less successful or was more or less promoted was also regarded. It came out that Latin American countries had several strong issues that were impediments to the integration processes. Those were conflicts up to wars between countries and a lack of political commitment. The following chapter, which examined integration theories applied in Europe and Latin America, complements those reasons. In Latin America politicians mainly determined integration processes whereas in Europe technicians also have a say. The application of different theoretical approaches on the integration processes was fruitful in finding several not instantly obvious explanations why integration went how it went. Three theoretical approaches were given as examples that they can be and are applied successfully in regions other than Europe. Those were neo-funtionalism, intergovernmentalism and constructivism. Those different approaches have the advantage that they offer different views on a matter. Some analysts of regional integration took on various of those views or approaches to make the outcome more valuable. It was found that Latin American countries were much more protectionist with respect to their sovereignty as European countries who went the way of sharing sovereignty. That integration in Latin America took place anyway was due to informal bounds such as friendships between the meeting persons of the institutions created within the integration process, but very much more because of power considerations. A big economic community has much more weight against economic giants such as the US and the EU. The EU as a unique organization can be was compared with other organizations and their integration processes. Finally, theories mostly developed because of the events in Europe can be and are also successfully applied in Latin America.

Bibliography

Aufteilung der Zuständigkeiten innerhalb der Europäischen Union. (n.a.). Retrieved March 12, 2012 from Europa.eu: http://europa.eu/legislation_summaries/institutional_affairs/treaties/lisbon_treaty/ai0020_de.htm

BBC News. Retrieved April 8, 2012 from Mercosur (Common Market of the South) - profile: http://news.bbc.co.uk/2/hi/americas/5195834.stm

Chapman, A. (January 1994). Retrieved April 9, 2012 from Free Trade in Latin America and the Caribbean: http://publications.gc.ca/Collection-R/LoPBdP/BP/bp372-e.htm#C. MERCOSUR(txt)

Checkel, J. T. (2006). Social Construction and Integration. In M. Eilstrup-Sangiovanni, *Debates on European Integration* (p. 406-419). New York: Palgrave Macmillan.

Christiansen, T., Jorgensen, K. E., & Wiener, A. (1999). The social construction of Europe. *Journal of European Public Policy , 6*, p. 528-544.

Das Gesicht Europas wandelt sich – Fall der Berliner Mauer. (n.a.). Retrieved March 12, 2012 from Europa.eu: http://europa.eu/about-eu/eu-history/1980-1989/index_de.htm

Diez, T. (2006). 'Speaking Europe': The Politics of Integration Discourse. In M. Eilstrup-Sangiovanni, *Debates on European Integration* (p. 420-436). New York: Palgrave Macmillan.

EEC. (n.a.). Retrieved March 12, 2012 from Europa-Summaries of European Legislation: http://europa.eu/legislation_summaries/institutional_affairs/treaties/treaties_eec_en.htm

Eilstrup-Sangiovanni, M. (2006). *Debates on European Integration.* New York: Palgrave Macmillan.

Encyclopedia.com. (n.a.). Retrieved March 17, 2012 from Social Constructivism: http://www.encyclopedia.com/topic/Social_constructionism.aspx

Encyclopedia69.com. (n.a.). Retrieved March 17, 2012 from http://www.encyclopedia69.com/eng/d/transactionalism/transactionalism.htm

Eu Politics. (n.a.). Retrieved March 21, 2012 from Social Constructivism: http://testpolitics.pbworks.com/w/page/24691740/Social%20%20Constructivism

EUFOR. Retrieved March 12, 2012 from http://www.euforbih.org

EUFOR. Retrieved April 9, 2012 from www.eufor.org

European Union. Retrieved April 8, 2012 from Countries: http://europa.eu/about-eu/countries/index_en.htm

Gómez-Mera, L. (2005). Explaining Mercosur's survival: strategic sources of Argentine-Brazilian convergence. *Journal of Latin American Studies* , *37*, p. 109-140.

Haas, E. (2006). Does Constructivism subsume Neofunctionalism. In M. Eilstrup-Sangiovanni, *Debates on European Integration* (p. 437-446). New York: Palgrave Macmillan.

Hansen, R. D. (2006). Regional Integration: Reflections on a Decade of Theoretical Efforts. In M. Eilstrupp-Sangiovanni, *Debates on European Integration* (p. 160-178). New York: Palgrave Macmillan.

Malamud, A. (November 2010). Latin American Regionalism and EU Studies. *European Integration* , *32*, p. 637 - 657.

Moravcsik, A. (n.a.). *Princeton*. Retrieved March 21, 2012 from Bringing Constructivist Integration Theory Out of the Clouds yet?: http://www.princeton.edu/~amoravcs/library/clouds.pdf

Risse, T., & Wiener, A. (1999). 'Something Rotten' and the Social Construction of Social Constructivism: A Comment of Comments. *Journal of European Public Policy* , *6* (5), p. 775-82.

Rosamond, B. (2006). The Future of European Studies: Integration Theory, EU Studies and Social Science. In Eilstrup-Sangiovanni, *Debates on European Integration* (p. 448-460). New York: Palgrave Macmillan.

Rueda-Junquera, F. (February 2006). From European Integration Model: Lessons for the Central American Common Market.

Sánchez Sánchez, R. A. (2003). *iadb.org*. Retrieved April 7, 2012 from The Central American Integration System as the Outcome of Asymmetrical Bargaining between States: an Intergovernmental Perspective of Regional Integration: http://www.iadb.org/intal/aplicaciones/uploads/publicaciones/i_INTAL_IYT_19_2003_Sanchez.pdf

Schmuck, O. (n.a.). *Bundeszentrale für politische Bildung*. Retrieved March 11, 2012 from Motive, Leitbilder und Etappen der europäischen Einigung : http://www.bpb.de/publikationen/5SLSCV,0,0,Motive_Leitbilder_und_Etappen_der_europ%E4ischen_E inigung.html

SICA Central American Integration System. Retrieved April 8, 2012 from Member States: http://www.sica.int/miembros/miembros_en.aspx?IdEnt=401&Idm=2&IdmStyle=2

SICE - Foreign Trade Information System. Retrieved April 9, 2012 from Central American Common Market: http://www.sice.oas.org/SICA/bkgrd_e.asp

Smith, S. (1999). Social Constructivism and European Studies: A Reflectivist Critique. *Journal of European Public Policy* , *4* (6), p. 482-91.

Summaries of European Legislation. (n.a.). Retrieved March 12, 2012 from Europa.eu: http://europa.eu/legislation_summaries/institutional_affairs/treaties/treaties_ecsc_en.htm

Viotti, P. R., & Kauppi, M. V. (2009). *International Relations Theory*. New York: Longman Pearson.

Warrick, W. R. (n.a.). *George Mason University*. From Constructivism: Pre-historical to Post-modern: http://mason.gmu.edu/~wwarrick/Portfolio/Products/constructivism.html abgerufen

Wiener, A., & Diez, T. (2003). *Uni Münster*. Retrieved March 23, 2012 from Beiträge des Arbeitskreises „Integrationsforschung" zum DVPW-Kongress „Stand und Perspektiven der Integrationsforschung" Integrationstheorien aus vergleichender Perspektive: Best Cases und Test Cases: https://www.uni-muenster.de/Politikwissenschaft/Doppeldiplom/docs/Integrationstheorien.pdf

Wirtschaftswoche. Retrieved April 9, 2012 from Schuldenkrise: http://www.wiwo.de/themen/Schuldenkrise